CARtoons

BY ANDY SINGER

WITH RANDY GHENT

FOREWORD BY JANE HOLTZ KAY

PUBLISHED BY

a project of World Carfree Network
London • Prague • Sydney • New York

CARTOONS

ISBN 80-238-7020-3

Printed and bound in the Czech Republic by Pematisk, Prague.

Published by
Car Busters Press, c/o World Carfree Network
Krátká 26, 100 00 Prague 10, Czech Republic
tel: +(420) 274-810-849 - fax: +(420) 274-772-017
info@carbusters.org - www.carbusters.org

 **ANDY SINGER** is a nomadic starving artist, who has lived in Berkeley, California; New York City; Boston; and St. Paul, Minnesota. He was married in a car-free wedding, riding off to his honeymoon on a bicycle. Until recently he supplemented his cartooning income with odd jobs such as photocopying and house painting, now abandoned in the hopes of filching off his wife's excellent teaching salary.

 **RANDY GHENT** is an American-born, Prague-based co-director of World Carfree Network. He divides his time between a modern fifth-floor apartment and a gypsy wagon without electricity or running water. There the apple and walnut trees enable him to eat breakfast without getting out of bed, let alone driving a car. He occasionally travels abroad but avoids countries where his name means "Horny Gentleman."

JANE HOLTZ KAY, making a cameo appearance in this book, is architecture and planning critic for *The Nation* and author of *"Lost Boston"* and *"Asphalt Nation: How the Automobile Took Over America and How We Can Take It Back,"* thus actually earning a living wage through writing. Not that we're jealous...

Contents

FOREWORD

BY JANE HOLTZ KAY

Stop that car! Follow that cartoon! Or, to invoke Andy Singer in the first edition of this book: follow that CARtoon.

And so he did, to the joy of followers who, like me, relish the chance to actually see the car culture lambasted in his visciously delicious caricatures.

The images didn't send the world into under-drive but enough followers grabbed a copy to exhaust the supply. So here we are again. As car gluttony does ever-enlarging mischief (think Iraq oil war and CO_2 emissions), Andy and World Carfree Network's Car Busters Press follow their sell-out first edition to continue to spread the word.

The inspired images of the first edition, plus a few additions, display this delightfully mean-spirited take on our car gluttony with Andy's sometimes surreal, sometimes sarcastic sense of humor—as dark and bold as his art. His mordant, mischievous outlook takes on the enemy and reminds us that you can hoist the car by its own petard. Alas, the last three years have actually seen a regression, with China and other accelerating car consumers entering the hypermobility race.

Considering the surreally comic implications of the fact that America's car population is growing at six times the rate of its human population, one wonders why it doesn't inspire humor on all fronts. But don't look at this book as a horror show or comic book. The words and statistics that fill its pages are informative and useful, a true-to-life tale amplifying Andy's art.

"Olympic Gold Medalist Tara Lipinski is turning 'Sweet Sixteen' and, like many teenagers, is looking forward to the day she can drive a car. With her mind on the dream, Tara takes a look at Autoweb.com, the biggest automotive dealer on-line. 'I travel a lot [by car], so doing things on-line makes sense because I don't have much time,' said Lipinski. 'The Autoweb.com site is really fun and a real quick way of looking at all my favorite cars from Chevrolet.'"

- Autoweb.com advertisement

I came upon Andy and his cartoons though a mutual friend in the anti-car culture, a growing body of folks who range from environmentalists to every-day would-be walkers. Andy had acquired his early anti-auto impulses from reading what Robert Moses did to maul New York, and could see plenty of the same even in our shared city of Boston, the so-called Hub, a sometimes kick-tire community where you can get around on two feet or two wheels or two rails.

Visualizing, or envisioning, as the New Age hawkers call it, is a powerful tool. And our car culture invites it. As the automobile becomes more implicated in climate change, Andy's humorous thrusts take on an ever darker cast. One activist describes driving as throwing a one-pound bag of carbon out the window every mile.

More happily, this collection of comic art shows the even wider visual range of opposition. "The Road to Hell," as Andy captions one drawing, is "Paved." And almost four years since this book made its way into thirty countries on five continents, the need is even greater.

The cartoonist who penned the words to this music and Car Busters Press, which supports its ongoing life in this second edition for an ever-enlarging audience, deserve 90-mile-an-hour applause. Or, should we say three-mile-an-hour accolades (the pace of the pedestrian), to keep us from what Andy calls "CARmageddon."

With quotes and statistics, this book continues this journey through Autoland and nimbly digests our travails with this devilish instrument of toxins and pollutants, of sprawl and ecological disaster. Anyone who cares about the fate of our warming, asphalted earth where vehicle-spewn gas changes the climate, will savor and, hopefully, find inspiration in this splendid CARtoon attack, renewed for an enlarging audience. ∎

Jane Holtz Kay

Boston, USA, Sept. 2004

Jane Holtz Kay, author of "Asphalt Nation" (1998), and architecture critic for The Nation, is currently writing "Last Chance Landscape."

**"Above all, it is the young who succumb to this magic.
They experience the triumph of the motorcar with the full temperament of their impressionable hearts. It must be seen as a sign of the invigorating power of our people that they give themselves with such fanatic devotion to this invention, the invention which provides the basis and structure of our modern traffic."**

- Adolf Hitler

"A 1995 British study found that children are as dependent on cars as their parents, with 90% of girls and 75% of boys saying they would find it difficult to adjust their lifestyles without a car...By the time children reach age 13 it is too late, the children having been already absorbed into the car culture."

- Sina Arnold and Domenica Settle, "Hooked on Cars: Driving as Addiction," in Car Busters magazine no. 7, Winter 1999-2000

CARS R US

"**The motorcar must be exciting and create a desire and not become mere transportation, or we will have just a utility, and people will spend their money on other things, such as swimming pools, boats, hi-fi sets, or European vacations.**"

- William Mitchell, former vice president of General Motors, 1965

There are *too many damn cars. I first recognized this in 1983, just after high school. A friend and I were unable to buy tickets for a rock concert on Long Island, New York, and had to sit outside the Nassau Coliseum for three hours, waiting for a ride home. Looking out, I saw seemingly endless parking lots surrounded by endless highways, streets and exit ramps, all of them filled with cars— thousands and thousands of cars. Amidst all this concrete, I couldn't see a single tree, a single bush*

or even a single blade of grass.

Once I became sensitized to cars, I realized that almost everything in North America is centered around the automobile. This is true of architecture, urban planning, socializing and even the basic procurement of goods and services. We have become a society in which the simplest human gatherings, like going to hear music or see a sporting event, require thousands of motor vehicles and miles of asphalt.

There are precious few places in America where you are not within

THE TRAFFIC REPORT

FOLKS, IT'S COMPLETELY HOPELESS. FOR GOD'S SAKE, **STOP DRIVING**!

HONK BEEP! BEEP! @!★彡彡 BEEP!

sight or sound of a road. Even the national forests aren't free of highways. The U.S. Forest Service has built 383,000 miles of roads to go with its 300,000 square miles of land.[1] Americans put in an average of ten 40-hour weeks behind the wheel each year[2] and spend over one-sixth of their income on cars.[3] If there is one thing more central to American life than the almighty dollar, it's the almighty car.

Images of cars and highways fill our literature, songs, movies and art, not just in America but world-wide. Books like "On the Road" by Jack Kerouac or "The Electric Kool-Aid Acid Test" by Tom Wolfe were among the first to romanticize driving and road trips. Old blues and early rock songs like "Route 66," "Brand New Cadillac," and "Goin' Mobile" further romanticized cars and highways for the postwar "Baby Boom" generation. Thousands of films and T.V. shows have focused on or predominantly featured cars and car chases: "Rebel Without a Cause," "American Graffiti," "Easy Rider," "Bullet," "The Dukes of Hazzard," the "James Bond" films, and at least half a dozen Burt Reynolds movies. The list goes on... All this pop culture, combined with relentless commercial advertising, has made cars an integral part of our personal identity. We have been taught to equate motor vehicles with wealth, power, romance, rebellion and freedom.

Now, everywhere I go in the world, I see cars—millions and millions of cars—in Rome, Guatemala City, Kuala Lumpur, Bombay and Beijing. Everywhere there are huge traffic jams and poor air quality. The number of motor vehicles in the world is growing three times faster than the population. At current growth rates, it will top one billion by the year 2025.[4]

Look around you. How many cars can you see from your office, house or apartment? How many go by each minute, each hour, each day? ■

---

1 National Forest Service, "Roads Analysis: Informing Decisions About Managing the National Forest Transportation System," Misc. report FS 643, Washington DC, 1999. <www.fs.fed.us/eng/road_mgt/01titlemain.pdf>.

2 U.S. Department of Transportation, "Summary of Travel Trends," National Personal Transportation Survey 1995. Washington, DC, 1999, Table #14. Available in print or on the web at: <www-cta.ornl.gov/npts/1995/DOC/trends_report.pdf>.

GREAT CITIES
OF THE WORLD

| ROME | PARIS |
| MADRID | NEW YORK |

SINGER

3 U.S. Bureau of the Census, *Statistical Abstract of the United States: 1999*, Washington DC, 1998, Table #738. Based on 1997 U.S. Bureau of Labor Statistics, the average American household allots $6,457 for "transportation." Subtracting its annual average expenditure for public transport of $393, yields a total expenditure of $6,064 per year on cars and related expenses (out of an annual, after-tax household income of $34,819).

4 Iain Carson, "Living With The Car," a survey by *The Economist*, June 22, 1996, pp. 52-54.

COMING SOON, TO A PLANET NEAR YOU...

FUTURISTIC SOCIETY #43:

A WORLD IN WHICH EVERYTHING IS IN TRAILERS, R.V.S OR MOBILE HOMES. THERE ARE NO FIXED BUILDINGS OR STRUCTURES OF ANY KIND, JUST ROADS, PAVEMENT, PARKING AND R.V. HOOKUPS. ALL COMMUNICATION IS BY CELLULAR PHONE.

SCHOOL

RESTAURANT

T.V. OR POLICE STATION

FEDERAL BUILDING

BANK WITH ATM IN BACK

ICE CREAM

GUY TRYING TO RETURN A LIBRARY BOOK

WIDE LOAD!

LIBRARY

SINGER

"The motor vehicle, that fun-filled, purring, and devilishly fast factory on wheels, has changed our entire public and social life in a few short decades; it has made people more mobile, distances shorter, usable land more extensive, besides having wrought a powerful transformation on the technical organization of work methods...The revolutionary automobile will serve the cause of the revolutionary working class."

- *Metallarbeiter (Metal Worker), #10, 1930*

"The new landmarks were not office towers or monuments or city halls or libraries or museums but 7-Eleven stores. In giving directions, people would say, 'You take the service road down past the 7-Eleven, and then...'"

- Tom Wolfe, "A Man in Full," 1998

IT'S A... DRIVE-THRU LIFE!

...HECK, YOU NEVER HAVE TO LEAVE YOUR CAR...

"In European communities auto use is generally between 30% and 48% of all trips; transit comprises between 11% and 26% of all trips; and pedestrian/bike trips are from 33% to 50% of the total. In comparison, the U.S. average mode split is 86% via auto, 8% walking, 3% bike and 3% transit. In the U.S., the commute itself constitutes only one-quarter of all car trips. Over 40% of car trips are for shopping, social or recreational purposes."

- Peter Calthorpe, "The Next American Metropolis," 1993; statistical abstract

AUTOEROTICISM

CAR WITH BRA

SINGER

CAR WITH BRA, STOCKINGS & PANTIES

"I love cars. I love cars of all shapes and sizes. Cars are a good thing...I also love roads. I have always loved roads."

- *Robert Key, former British Minister of Roads, 1998*

ROMANTICIZED OBJECTS

"Many men have had love affairs with their cars. Buster Mitchell wanted to make it official. Jilted by his girlfriend, a bereft Mitchell decided he wanted to marry his true love, his 1996 Mustang GT... It was sometime after he listed his fiancee's birthplace as 'Detroit,' her father as 'Henry Ford,' and her blood type as '10-W-40' that his plans sputtered."

- Associated Press, March 1999

"High speeds for all means that everybody has less time for himself as the whole society spends a growing slice of its time budget on moving people... The allure of speed has deceived the passenger into accepting the promises made by an industry that produces capital intensive traffic. He is convinced that high-speed vehicles have allowed him to progress beyond the limited autonomy he enjoyed when moving under his own power...The passenger who agrees to live in a world monopolized by transport becomes a harassed, overburdened consumer of distances whose shape and length he can no longer control."

- Ivan Illich, "Energy and Equity," 1973

"'Urban planning' is an indefensible euphemism. Urban planners do not plan. They follow along behind the parade of those who do—the land developers. The role of the professional planners is to sweep up and organize the dung."

- Stanley Hart and Alvin Spivak, "The Elephant in the Bedroom," 1992

"The only way you could tell you were leaving one community and entering another was when the franchises started repeating and you spotted another 7-Eleven, another Wendy's, another Costco, another Home Depot."

- Tom Wolfe, "A Man in Full," 1998

INCARCERATED

SINGER

"The product that has so strongly shaped the urban world we live in, and brought such wealth and such pleasure, is now seen by many as... a blessing turning into a curse." - *The Economist*

Highway commissioners and government officials who advocate building urban freeways should be forced to live next to one. It's an eye-opening experience.

In the summer of 1991, I moved into an apartment in a run-down section of Oakland, California, 100 yards from the MacArthur Freeway interchange. This is where Interstate 580 meets Highway 24—six layers of overlapping highways on massive concrete pillars. On traffic reports, it is referred to simply as "The Maze."

Living next to this monstrosity, I came to see how highways actually destroy neighborhoods and whole cities by cutting pedestrians off from goods and services and by polluting them with ugliness, noise and smog. I came to see how freeways further gut cities by enabling urban flight which, in turn, fuels suburban sprawl and the destruction of rural land.

In his 1999 State of the Union Address, President Bill Clinton remarked that, in the U.S., "seven thousand acres of farmland and open space are lost (to sprawl) every day."[1] Indeed, since childhood, I've watched the suburbs of Orinda and Walnut Creek grow dramatically, even as the inner city of Oakland decayed and shrank. Cars and highways have enabled this to happen, and it's high time people faced up to the tremendous economic and social costs that automobiles impose on society.

The economic costs are staggering. In my country, the federal, state and local tax expenditures for highways total over US$100 billion. Then there's the $3,100 per year, on average, which each U.S. citizen spends to own and maintain an automobile (insurance, gas, oil, maintenance and depreciation).[2] For America's fleet of 200 million cars, this cost amounts to over $600 billion per year!

This is just the beginning. There are the huge costs associated with the 35 million U.S. motor vehicle accidents each year. There are the medical costs of air pollution, which the American Lung Association computes at $50 billion annually. There is the cost to businesses for providing subsidized parking and access space to customers and employees. There's the cost of wasted fuel and lost productivity, in the over 3.5 billion hours per year Americans spend stuck in traffic.[3] There are the costs of wars that must be fought to ensure access to foreign oil. Finally, there are the incalculable "external" costs of global warming, pollution and habitat destruction associated with motor vehicles. Some say we spend 18% of our GDP on transportation (as compared to 9% for Japan).[4] The real figure could be much higher.

Then there are the social costs. In contrast to the romantic images of advertising and pop culture, increased "automobility" has meant a loss of community, causing further distancing of social groups and alienation. This social alienation is true for all Americans, but especially the third of the population who are unable to drive. Suburban youth and suburban elderly are isolated in spread out, single-family homes. Unable to socialize or even get around without a car, they must be shuttled to school or recreational events by those who can drive. Often, families must drive 30 minutes just to get a quart of milk or a loaf of bread! All this driving becomes a stressful chore, a waste of precious time and life. I've seen

---

1 From United States President Clinton's state of the Union Address 1/19/99 ("All communities face a preservation challenge, as they grow, and green space shrinks. Seven thousand acres of farmland and open space are lost every day...").

2 U.S. Bureau of the Census— Statistical Abstract of the United States: 1999 (119th edition) Washington DC, 1998, Table #738, Table #740 and Table #1027.

Based on US Bureau of Labor Statistics from 1997, the average American household allots $6,457 for "Transportation." Subtracting its annual average expenditure for public transport of $393, yields a total expenditure of $6,064 per year on cars and their related expenses. Since there are 106 million households and 208 million motor vehicle registrations, this means there are 1.96 cars per household. Dividing $6,064 by 1.96 yields $3,094 per registered vehicle.

3 Texas Transportation Institute, "2004 Annual Mobility Report," National Congestion Tables, Table #2 (Components of the Congestion Problem, 2002 Urban

suburbanites and other commuters made prisoners of their cars by traffic and this necessity to drive. This prison-like frustration breeds "road rage" and aggressive driving.

With aggressive driving and other distractions come traffic accidents and their resulting injuries and fatalities. In 1996, over six million Americans were injured (some severely) and 42,000 died in car accidents.[5] In my 38 years of life, many of my close friends and acquaintances have been injured or died in car accidents. My third grade teacher and my friend Duffy Booth both died. My friends Roger, Joan, Pete, Terry and many others have all been severely injured. It seems like every day I hear about another celebrity or public figure being killed or maimed by a car.

We have created a mechanized concrete environment that is increasingly unfriendly and hazardous to

CAR TRICKS

Cars will "eliminate a greater part of the nervousness, distraction, and strain of modern metropolitan life."

- prediction, Scientific American magazine, 1899

human beings. As we spend more and more time trapped behind the wheels of our cars, as ever more land is bulldozed and made into strip malls and parking lots, the experts tell us our "standard of living" is increasing dramatically. But what about our quality of life? ∎

Area Totals), <http://mobility.tamu.edu/ums>; U.S. Bureau of the Census— Statistical Abstract of the United States: 1998, Washington DC, 1998, Tables #1027 and #1040.

Alternatively, the TTI "1999 Annual Mobility Report" computes the average annual time spent by drivers stuck in traffic at "34 hours per driver." Multiply this number (34 hours) by the total number of licensed drivers from Statistical Abstract (182,709,000), and you get over "6.2 billion hours stuck in traffic." Similarly, multiplying the average annual congestion

cost per driver ($630) by the total number of licensed drivers (182,709,000) yields an estimated annual cost of traffic congestion of about "$115 billion."

4 Walter Hook, "Are Bicycles Making Japan More Competitive?" Sustainable Transport #2 (New York, Institute For Transportation and Development Policy) Summer 1993. <www.itdp.org/ST2/ST2japan.doc>.

5 U.S. Bureau of the Census— Statistical Abstract of the United States: 1998 (118th edition) Washington DC, 1998, Tables #1041 and #1043.

"It is apparent in hindsight that the utopia of mass motorization rested on the illusion that the pleasure of early motorists could add up to a general mobility prosperity for the masses. Yet this utopian projection failed to consider that the desires of individuals—in a space subject to limited enlargement— will necessarily run into and diminish each other...
The automobile belongs to a class of commodities that cannot be multiplied at will. Because its attraction requires the exclusion of the masses, the democratization of car ownership destroys its advantages."

- Wolfgang Sachs, "For the Love of the Automobile," 1984

AUTOMOBILES:

"Given the tremendous success of the automobile, one might expect a virtual consensus that such as achievement should be preserved and enhanced. One might expect the experts to recognize the automobile's virtues as much as the people and concentrate their efforts on making it even better. But no! In discussions of transportation policy, a growing number of very vocal critics and analysts see the automobile not as a solution but as a problem, and auto policy not as a success but as a failure. They want Americans to take public transit, ride share, pedal bikes, or walk—in other words to abandon the very same cars that provide such mobility and a sense of empowerment and equality."

- James A. Dunn, Jr., "Driving Forces: The Automobile, Its Enemies and the Politics of Mobility," 1998

OUR TECHNOLOGICAL UTOPIA

"If a society opts for high energy consumption, its social relations must be dictated by technocracy and will be equally degrading whether labeled capitalist or socialist."

- Ivan Illich, "Energy and Equity," 1973

"Unlike the vacuum cleaner, the radio, or the bicycle, which retain their use value when everyone has one, the car, like a villa by the sea, is only desirable and useful insofar as the masses don't have one. That is how in both conception and original purpose the car is a luxury good. And the essence of luxury is that it cannot be democratized. If everyone can have luxury, no one gets any advantages from it. On the contrary, everyone diddles, cheats, and frustrates everyone else, and is diddled, cheated, and frustrated in return."

- André Gorz, "L'Idéologie Sociale de la Bagnole," in Le Sauvage, Sept.-Oct. 1973

DRIVE TO WORK / WORK TO DRIVE

"The typical American male devotes more than 1,600 hours a year to his car. He sits in it while it goes and while it stands idling. He parks it and searches for it. He earns the money to put down on it and to meet the monthly installments. He works to pay for petrol, tolls, insurance, taxes and tickets. He spends four of his sixteen waking hours on the road or gathering his resources for it...The model American puts in 1,600 hours to get 7,500 miles: less than five miles per hour."

- Ivan Illich, "Energy and Equity," 1973

"In the mechanized, high-energy system developed during the last two centuries...there is only one efficient speed, *faster;* only one attractive destination, *farther away;* only one desirable size, *bigger;* only one rational quantitative goal, *more.*"

- Louis Mumford, "The Pentagon of Power," 1970

"People who live in sprawling suburbs where they must drive to school, to work or to the store are likely to weigh six pounds more than their counterparts in more walkable cities..."

- *"Suburban Sprawl Adds Health Concerns, Studies Say,"*
The New York Times, August 31, 2003

"Remember the Gulf War... We fought a war over oil, to keep
Saddam Hussein from going into Kuwait, from going into
Saudi Arabia and controlling the world supply of oil."

- Frank Murkowski (Republican), former U.S. senator, now governor
of Alaska, on National Public Radio, March 15, 2001

"Despite funding the lion's share of highways and street infrastructure in major U.S. cities with their state and local tax dollars, as many as two-thirds of city dwellers don't even own cars since keeping them is prohibitively expensive."

- Robert Caro, "The Power Broker," 1974

I LIVE IN A LITTLE HOUSE UNDERNEATH THE MACARTHUR FREEWAY INTERCHANGE.

ANYONE WHO SAYS, "PUTTING HIGHWAYS THROUGH URBAN NEIGHBORHOODS IS A GOOD IDEA," NEEDS THEIR HEAD EXAMINED.

IMAGINE LIVING UNDER THE CONSTANT DRONING NOISE OF A FREEWAY—DAY IN AND DAY OUT—HAVING YOUR HOUSE SHAKE AS BIG TRUCKS AND BUSES RUMBLE BY...

OR HAVING YOUR WINDOWSILLS AND PORCHES COVERED WITH BLACK TIRE DUST AND YOUR GROUND FILLED WITH LEAD.

FORGET VEGETABLE GARDENING NEAR A FREEWAY. IT'S JUST A TICKET TO SLOW LEAD POISONING.

AN EXAMINATION OF URBAN AREAS SHOWS HOW FREEWAYS HAVE DESTROYED NEIGHBORHOODS

"Beyond a certain speed, motorized vehicles create remoteness which they alone can shrink. They create distances for all and shrink them for only a few...

IN **WEST OAKLAND CALIFORNIA,** THE CYPRESS FREEWAY TOOK AN ALREADY MARGINAL AREA AND TURNED IT INTO A GHETTO, POLLUTING IT AND CUTTING IT OFF FROM THE REST OF THE CITY.

FREEWAYS IN **SAN FRANCISCO** DID THE SAME THING TO HUNTERS POINT.

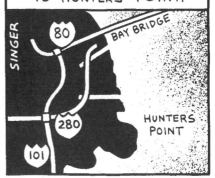

THE **SOUTH BRONX** IN NEW YORK CITY... SAME STORY.

NORTHERN NEW JERSEY!!

DON'T LET YOUR NEIGHBORHOOD BE DEVOURED BY

...THE FREEWAY MONSTER

The new expressway expands Chicago, but it sucks those who are well wheeled away from a downtown that decays into a ghetto."

- Ivan Illich, "Energy and Equity," 1973

"Universal mobility takes the magic out of distance...The masters of space
and time awaken to find themselves slaves of distance and haste."

- Wolfgang Sachs, "For the Love of the Automobile," 1984

CARNAGE

"New! Practical! Gas-powered motorcar, patented in all industrial countries. Entirely supercedes the horse and wagon... Always starts right up... very low operating costs...comfortable and totally safe!"

- Benz & Co., first automobile prospectus in Germany, 1888

While many debate the quality of life issues, one thing is certain: from an environmental point of view, cars are decimating the planet. Motor vehicles are one of the biggest sources of pollution and environmental destruction in the world. Almost half of all petroleum produced in the world is consumed by cars. Half of the toxic air pollution, a third of the smog and nearly a third of all greenhouse gases are produced by cars. But emissions are just the tip of the (melting) iceberg. In the U.S., cars account for at least a quarter of the contaminants in waterways, in the form of acid rain, leaking gas station tanks, batteries, tanker spills, runoff and home mechanics' dumping oil.[1]

From the foam and plastic in its seats to the petroleum in its tires, each car is a small pollution factory. Several tons of waste and 1.2 billion cubic yards of polluted air are generated in its manufacture alone! During its lifetime, on the road, each car produces another 1.3 billion cubic yards of polluted air and scatters an additional 40 pounds of worn tire particles, brake debris and worn road surface into the atmosphere.[2] This black soot or "tire dust" contaminates our lungs and waterways. I watched it accumulate on my windowsills and

D E V E L O P M E N T

porches in Oakland, California. It's no wonder that children who live near freeways in poor neighborhoods have higher rates of asthma.

Ever-growing piles of junked tires pose a toxic waste problem. Now numbering almost one billion in the U.S. alone, these tires foul ground water with zinc and heavy metals and often catch fire. Consequently, they are very hard to dispose of. Efforts at reclaiming oil from them, recycling them into other products, and adding them to road material, while better than nothing, have had minimal impact. In some cases, these efforts have made their environmental impacts even worse.

In the U.S., motorists kill and maim nearly 400 million animals per year—more than hunters and experimenters combined! Only meat eaters take a larger toll. Worse, of all the killers, cars are the most indiscriminate. Along with deer and countless other common animals, motor vehicles also kill many endangered species. Florida's endangered black bears, Florida's panthers, and northern Idaho and southern British Columbia's endangered caribou have all been devastated by cars.[3]

In part because of road kill, highways effectively divide habitats. A ring road around a coastal city means animals within the ring can't get out to feed or mate with those on the outside. A major highway bisecting a forest or wilderness area has the same effect. The result is a shrinking of the gene pool, decreasing the chances that a species will survive a disease, drought or severe environmental change. For precisely this reason, roads are considered a major threat to the remaining giant pandas.[4]

---

1 Michael Brower and Warren Leon, _The Consumer's Guide to Effective Environmental Choices_ (New York, Three Rivers Press, 1999) pp. 51-56. Cf: Union of Concerned Scientists, "Cars, Trucks and Air Pollution"/ "Cars, Trucks and Global Warming", (Cambridge, MA, 2004), <www.ucsusa.org/clean_vehicles/archive/ page.cfm?pageID=207> and <www.ucsusa.org/ clean_vehicles/cars_and_suvs/page.cfm?pageID=224>. Above figures do not include CO_2 emissions and pollution related to road construction, or vehicle production and disposal. For research on the latter, see Umwelt und Prognose-Institut Heidelberg, 1993 and <www.ilea.org>.

Then there's the pollution from maintaining roads. Salts and de-icing agents are used to keep northern roadways free of ice and snow. Besides corroding cars and rusting bridges and infrastructure, salts fill up wells and wetlands, salinizing ground water and blighting older trees and indigenous vegetation. Herbicides used to control roadside vegetation have a similar impact, contaminating soil and fouling ground water.

Finally, building highways has facilitated suburban development, bringing the environmental devas-tation wreaked by cars further into rural and wilderness areas. Even without the cars themselves, scientists believe that suburban sprawl may contribute to global warming, since asphalt often displaces trees and green spaces that absorb carbon dioxide and cool surface temperatures.

Certainly, sprawl encourages non-organic, agribusiness-style farming, concentrating and moving food farther from consumers. In America, the typical bite of food must now travel 1,400 miles to reach the dinner plate.[5] People are becoming increasingly dependent on petroleum just to eat! The American Farmland Trust estimates that between 1 and 1.5 million acres of U.S. farmland are consumed each year by sprawl. If the trend continues, this loss will damage the nation's ability to export foodstuffs and even to feed itself.

Like I said, you can debate whether cars improve or degrade our quality of life, but there is no debating this fact: If we don't stop building new cars and roads, our environment, and we who depend on it for life, are done for. ■

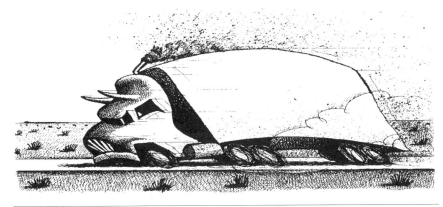

2 Jane Holtz Kay, Asphalt Nation, pp. 92-94.

3 Matthew Braunstein, "Driving Animals to Their Graves," Auto-Free Times, (Arcata, CA, Fossil Fuels Policy Action Institute), Spring 1996, pp. 12-13. (Figure based on Humane Society studies in the 1950s and 1970s, showing that over a million animals die each day on U.S. roads, inc. mammals, birds, reptiles and amphibians.)

4 Chris Catton, Pandas (New York, Facts on File Publications, 1990), pp. 118-119. Cf: National Geographic Society, Secrets of the Wild Panda, 1994, video.

5 Tracy Baxter, "The Real Cost of Globetrotting Food," Green Guide 64, February 1999, pp. 1-3.

"It is strange that people always want to shift responsibility for the frights they take and the accidents they suffer onto other people and that they abuse the automobile driver, who just happens to be there."

- keynote speaker, *Extraordinary Automobile Convention, Berlin, 1908*

WE'RE ALL BEING KILLED BY "SECONDHAND SMOKE"

CAR EXHAUST

SINGER

THE GREENHOUSE EFFECT

MOTORIZED LEMMINGS

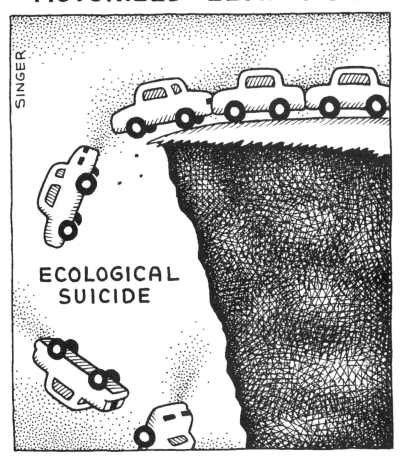

"There are two roads from where we are to technological maturity: one is the road of liberation from affluence; the other is the road of liberation from dependence. Both roads have the same destination: the social restructuring of space that offers to each person the constantly renewed experience that the center of the world is where he stands, walks and lives."

- Ivan Illich, "Energy and Equity," 1973

HIGHWAYS DIVIDE HABITATS

"Suburbia, where they tear out all the trees and then name streets after them."

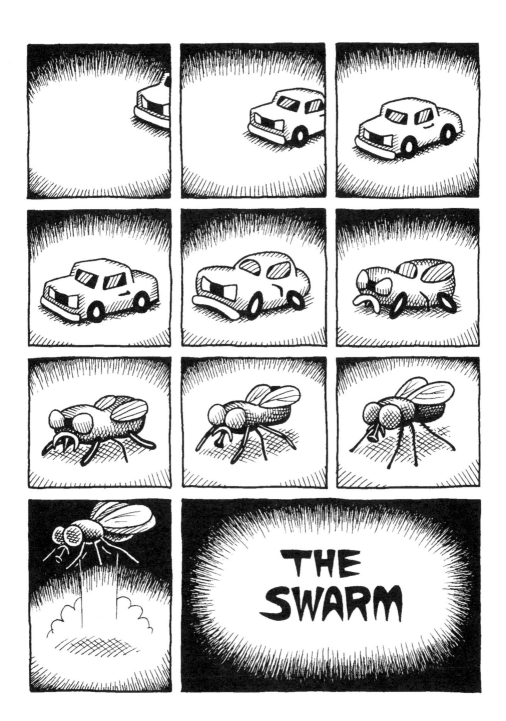

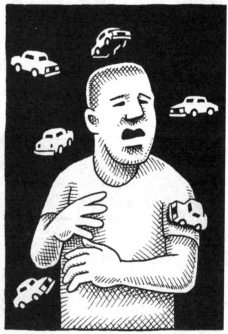

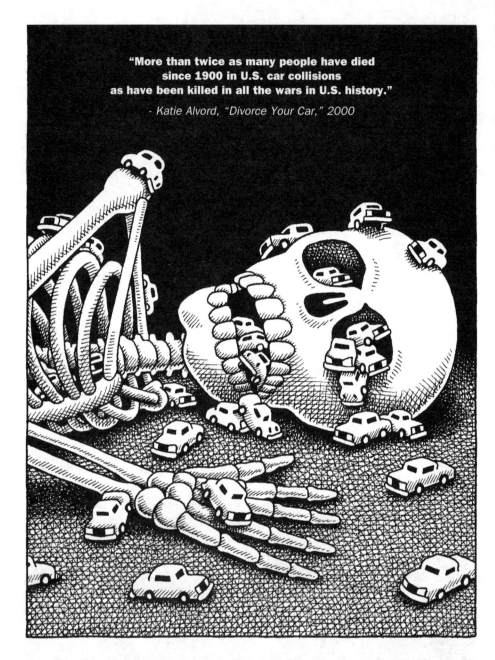

"More than twice as many people have died
since 1900 in U.S. car collisions
as have been killed in all the wars in U.S. history."

- Katie Alvord, "Divorce Your Car," 2000

"The mechanical carriage is here once and for all, and, however one might
persecute it, it will not die, because it corresponds to the logic
of economic progress and the needs of our time."

- L. Baundry de Saunier, "Fundamental Principles of Automobilism," 1902

CARMAGEDDON

(A SHORT HISTORY OF THE CAR)

How did we end up with all these cars? As with everything in life, the reasons are varied. Some are innocent, some utopian and some are selfish and evil.

To people at the beginning of the twentieth century, cars and internal combustion engines seemed less polluting than the piles of horse manure that filled many city streets. In America, cars and trucks also appealed to many (particularly rural people) who had experienced the monopolistic railroad practices of the late 1800s. Utopians like Henry Ford, Adolph Hitler and many far kinder and gentler folks preached of "democratizing" the automobile and of its potential to liberate society, both physically and spiritually. They constructed the early parkways and autobahns and were the first to mass produce cars. These idealist and utopian themes were then picked up and paraded about by auto manufacturers, oil companies and their advertisers and lobbyists, who said cars and buses would be cheaper and more efficient than trains and trolleys.

When lobbying and advertising didn't work, oil and car companies resorted to outright criminal activity. Led by General Motors, they secretly conspired to create National City Lines, a transit "front" company that took over and ripped up 100 commuter rail networks in 45 U.S. cities, replacing them with buses.

By the depression of the 1930s, intensive lobbying and advertising had produced a Works Project Administration and other U.S. government relief efforts that favored roads, bridges and tunnels for cars. To build these highway networks, governments created quasi-public agencies, often by issuing bonds.

These agencies or "authorities" were inherently anti-democratic. To this day, they function almost like independent sovereign states. They have the power of eminent domain (to seize private property), the power to levy taxes (tolls) and the power to govern and police their domains according to their own laws. Their directors are usually appointed by mayors, governors or presidents and, once appointed, they can be very hard to remove.

The ability to spend billions of dollars in federal and state funds gives highway agencies and their directors incredible political power. All this money represents thousands of jobs and huge profits for engineering and construction firms. Consequently, unions, trade associations and many other well-organized groups can be called upon to support highway projects. Politicians who oppose these projects can find themselves quickly voted out of office.

Since their creation in the 1930s and '40s, U.S. highway agencies, like giant living organisms, have tried to grow, feeding themselves with public tax money. By the late 1940s they had become a powerful lobby in government and were regularly advocating for and building huge automobile bridges, tunnels and freeways. Combined with car manufacturers and oil companies, they formed a giant American "Auto-Industrial Complex," which, by 1956, had produced The Interstate Highway Act, gas tax revenues and billions of dollars in additional federal and state subsidies.

When their bridges and highways began to fill with cars, the highway lobby built new roads and widened old ones, in the name of "reducing traffic" and "improving safety." When these new roads also filled up, officials assured the public that building still more roads would alleviate the problem. Today, American highways are as congested and accident-ridden as ever, yet highway agencies continue to promise that building even more roads will solve the problem. This is complete nonsense.

As early as the 1960s, traffic engineers found that more roads

1 Thomas Bass, "Road to Ruin," Discover, May 1992, pp. 56-61. Cf: Richard Arnott and Kenneth Small, "The Economics of Traffic Congestion," American Scientist (North Carolina Scientific Research Society), Volume 82, Sept.-Oct. 1994, pp. 446-455;

Anthony Downs, Stuck in Traffic, (Washington DC, Brookings Institution, 1992) pp. 26-34; Todd Litman, "Generated Traffic—Implications for Transport Planning," Victoria Transport Policy Institute, 1999, <www.vtpi.org/gentraf.pdf>.

just generated more traffic. Numerous studies and history itself now show that traffic expands to fill available road space until some tolerable level of congestion is reached. Engineers call this phenomenon "traffic generation," "The Downs-Thompson Paradox" or "Braess's Paradox." If new lanes are added to relieve

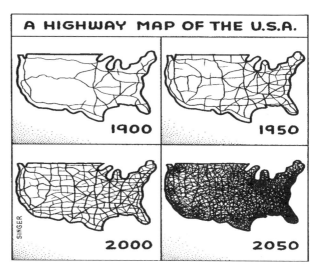

A HIGHWAY MAP OF THE U.S.A.

1900 1950 2000 2050

SINGER

road congestion, speed increases and trip times decrease, but demand also increases until you're back to the same congested roads.[1]

In general, building highways is an ineffective way to move large masses of people. An automobile lane can carry a maximum of just 1,500 cars per hour. By contrast, a single track of transit can carry 40,000 to 50,000 people per hour.[2] In July 1998, even the EPA ruled that "highway expansion increases driving," and (since cars affect air quality) it required that traffic generation be factored into Transportation Improvement Plans.[3] Certainly, I've seen this in Berkeley, California, where CALTRANS has widened Interstate 80 twice (to

five lanes in each direction), yet congestion is worse than ever.

As far as improving safety, widening and straightening roads only increases highway speeds, and speed kills. A pedestrian is 10 times more likely to be killed by a car going 30 mph than by one going 15 mph.[4] For drivers too, faster cars increase the risk of severe injury or death. You can achieve safety without straightening roads or ripping up trees.

So, no matter what country you live in, think about all this the next time some highway agency tells you they need to widen a road or build a new one to improve the flow of traffic. History has shown their promises to reduce traffic congestion are lies. Tell them they can go to hell! ∎

2 Robert A. Caro, The Power Broker, (New York, Vintage Books, 1974), p. 901.

3 Paul Wentworth, "EPA Rules Highway Expansion Increases Driving," Livable Places Update, Emerging Trends in Community Planning and Design, Sept. 1998,

<www.lgc.org/freepub/PDF/Land_Use/lpu/lpu_9809.pdf>.

4 Stephen H. Burrington and Veronika Thiebach, "Take Back Your Streets—How to Protect Your Communities From Asphalt and Traffic" (Boston, Conservation Law Foundation, 1998), <www.clf.org>.

TRAFFIC ISLAND
(LOS ANGELES, CALIFORNIA)

**"The Roman Emperor Hadrian insightfully observed:
'This luxury of speed destroys its own aim; a pedestrian makes
more headway than a hundred conveyances jammed end to end
along the twists and turns of the Sacred Way.' To the best of our
knowledge, this stands as the first traffic report."**

*- Sean Hayes, "Autobiography: An Alternative History of the Car"
in "Beyond the Car: Essays on the Auto Culture," 1995*

NOAH'S R.V.

"Not surprisingly, the Bible says nothing about cars or urban sprawl. However, one passage from Acts 8:29 reads: 'Go near and join thyself to this chariot.' This could conceivably be interpreted as a direct commandment against walking."

- *Sean Hayes, Ibid*

"Not only are the Chinese responsible for spaghetti and gunpowder, but they are also responsible for creating the very first self-propelled vehicles. According to the legend, the Chou Dynasty of 800 B.C. was the age of steam-powered 'fire carts.' However, lousy marketing and distribution, as well as poor dealer support, inhibited mass acceptance of these fire carts, and they quickly faded from use. Of course, most Western historians jealously dismiss the possibility that they ever existed."

- *Sean Hayes, Ibid*

"Each time you travel in your automobile the image of the Sacred Heart will remind you of your pledge of safe driving. And you will know that you and your traveling companions are under His protection."

- Father Bob Hess, Sacred Heart Auto League, Walls, Mississippi 38686

"Car culture has pervaded our very language: We 'invest' in airports and roads...
but we 'subsidize' public transit. Look at the numbers! in 1998, cars got
five times more U.S. federal money than transit." - *Andy*

A RIVER OF TRAFFIC
(AND ITS TRIBUTARIES)

"Just as horse-drawn vehicles once had to create paths and the railroad had to build rail lines, so must motorized transportation be granted the streets it needs. If in earlier times one attempted to measure people's relative standard of living according to kilometers of railway track, in the future one will have to plot the kilometers of streets suited to motor vehicle traffic."

- Adolph Hitler, February 11, 1933

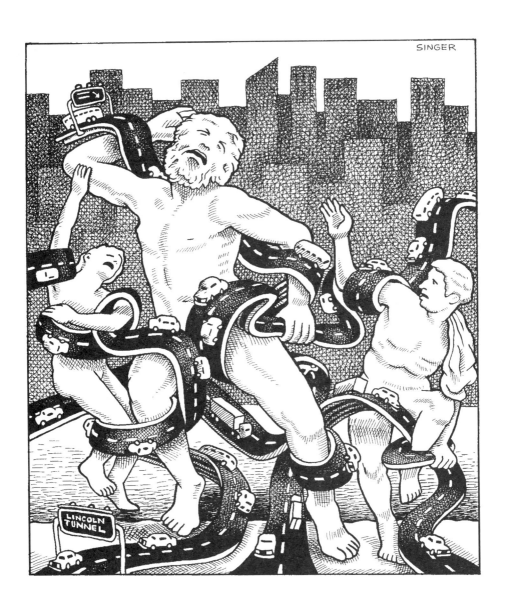

"As flawless and powerful as the National Socialist revolution itself, the highways will spread across the land. They are not to be a destruction of nature, the ugly product of a degenerate technology, but the supreme crowning of the landscape...It is not roads, then, that are to arise, but works of art— just as once the temples were built, and not huts; cathedrals, and not mere prayer houses; pyramids, and not tombstones. That is what the Führer wants. For the first time in the history of humanity, the Führer is elevating the street above the domain of the natural path and artificial road construction, and into the sphere of art."

- W. Bade, "Das Auto erobert die Welt: Biographie des Kraftwagens," 1938

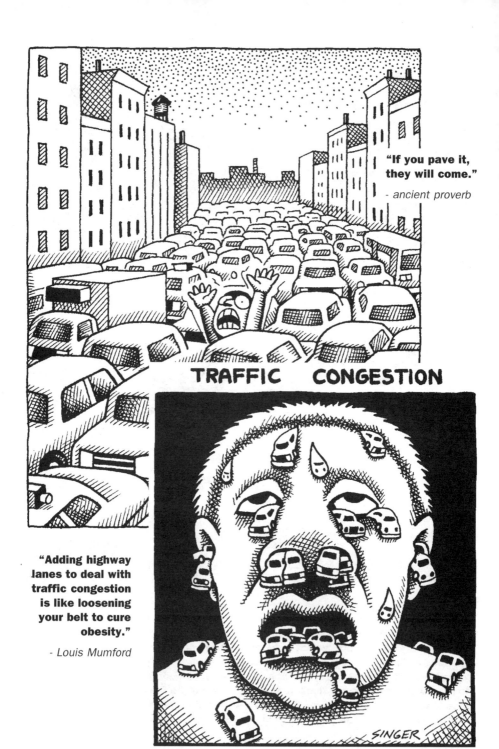

"If you pave it, they will come."

- *ancient proverb*

TRAFFIC CONGESTION

"Adding highway lanes to deal with traffic congestion is like loosening your belt to cure obesity."

- *Louis Mumford*

SINGER

"THE ROAD TO HELL IS PAVED WITH GOOD INTENTIONS"

THE ROAD TO HELL IS **PAVED.**

"The United States is covered by 38.4 million acres of roads and parking lots. Thirty to fifty percent of urban American land is paved over. Sixty percent of Los Angeles is paved. In Houston, Texas, the figure for the amount of asphalt is 30 car spaces per resident. A car [in America] requires on average 30 square meters of space at one's home, 30 square meters near one's destination, 60 square meters of road surface, and about 20 square meters to be sold, repaired and maintained. Each car thus requires a ground surface equivalent to that of a four-person apartment."

- Stephen Goddard, "Getting There," 1994; Jane Holtz Kay, "Asphalt Nation," 1997; Jean Robert, "Le Temps Qu'on Nous Vole," 1980

**"Their very numbers began to distill the poison
that blights the paradise they seek."**

- Frederick Law Olmsted, Jr., Detroit, 1905, on suburban flight

CARTELS

Chevron

"I'm passionate about the environment and the auto industry. I believe the two are compatible."

- Bill Ford, Jr., President, Ford Motor Company, 1999

With half a billion motor vehicles on the planet, it goes without saying that cars are big business. How big? The automobile and oil industries, which grew hand in hand during the twentieth century, now form the bedrock of the world's primary industries. Six of America's ten largest corporations are either auto or oil companies. According to the American Automobile Manufacturers Association, a fifth of the U.S. Gross Domestic Product is dependent on the auto industry. One out of six U.S. workers makes a living in an auto-related industry, producing cars, trucks, oil or highways, repairing cars, driving cars, parking cars, making parts or selling parts. More than 50% of the oil, 64% of the rubber, 33% of the iron, 27% of the aluminum and 20% of all electronics and carpeting goes into cars.[1] With annual sales of about US$1 trillion, the auto industry accounts for at least one in ten jobs in industrialized countries.[2]

Since markets in North America, Europe and Japan are experiencing slower growth rates than in the past, auto companies are scurrying to create and meet demand in places like China, India and Latin America. They are creating this "demand" much as they did in the United States—through advertising, and using their size and associations with other big businesses to influence local and national governments. Car manufacturers spend $14 billion a year on advertising and promotion in the U.S. alone.[3] That's more than the entire GDP of many developing nations...just on advertising! With this kind of money, they can

persuade governments to build highways, grant subsidies and favor auto-centric development. They can also insure a positive representation of highways and cars in the local media. Furthermore, car companies can influence the Agency for International Development, the IMF and the World Bank to fund road and highway construction abroad and promote U.S.-style, car-based transportation and urban planning. As a result of all this power and influence, car sales in non-Western

WARNING: MAY CAUSE OBESITY, GLOBAL WARMING AND FEELINGS OF EXTREME RAGE AND FRUSTRATION

$18,000

countries are projected to skyrocket. This would lead to a doubling of the world's car population (to over one billion) before the year 2030.[4] This will have devastating consequences for the environment.

The desire to produce and sell cars to new, "undeveloped" markets is one of the major forces driving the international "free trade" movement. The other major force is industry's desire to escape "First World" environmental and labor regulations. The Free Traders contend that their motivations are somehow altruistic—that the unregulated, free flow of industrial goods and capital will somehow be inherently good for society. This is

a lie. The automotive industry's real motivation is to sell as many cars and make as much profit as possible.

Environmental issues, labor conditions, and local quality of life are simply obstacles in the path to profit. Witness how Ford's new chairman, a self-proclaimed "environmentalist," has said Ford will continue to produce sport-utility vehicles even though they pose a safety and environmental hazard.[5] Witness the scandal at Firestone (linked to over 80 deaths).[6] Witness how the oil and auto industries continue to promote and sell leaded gasoline in Eastern Europe and the "Third World," despite overwhelming evidence of its extreme toxicity. Witness Exxon's failure to pay court-ordered damages in Alaska following the Valdez oil spill.[7] And observe Shell's role in the execution of eight community activists by the Nigerian government[8] or Texaco's racist employment policies.[9] These institutions are not going to behave themselves and work for the betterment of society. They must be strictly regulated and policed.

Besides, the automobile itself is inherently anti-environmental. While better than nothing, fuel cell, electric or hybrid cars won't change the

1 "Material Usage By The Automotive Industry," Motor Vehicles Facts and Figures 1996 (Detroit, MI, American Automobile Manufacturers Association, 1996); Jane Holtz Kay, Asphalt Nation, pg. 123.

2 Iain Carson, "Living With The Car," A Survey by The Economist, June 22, 1996, pp. 52-53.

3 "100 Leading National Advertisers," Advertising Age (Midwest Region Ed.), Sept. 27, 1998, p. S3.

4 Iain Carson, "Living With The Car," A Survey by The Economist, June 22, 1996, pp. 52-54.

5 Keith Bradsher, "Ford is Conceding S.U.V. Drawbacks," New York Times, May 12, 2000, p. A1.

multitude of other problems that cars create (like sprawl, habitat destruction, gridlock, tire fires and waste disposal problems). Cars have become a public health hazard. Each year they kill or maim millions of people and irreparably destroy our environment.

Yet we accept this idea of "free trade"—that auto makers or other industries have some inalienable right to promote and sell their goods and make as much profit as possible. This is madness! Trade should be "free" only to the degree that the parties involved are respecting health, labor and the environment, and only to the degree that the commodity they are trading is socially and ecologically sustainable. As Michael Moore says, General Motors could make a profit selling crack cocaine, but we don't allow it since we realize that cocaine is harmful to society. So we pass national and international drug-trafficking laws to strictly regulate its sale, use and distribution.

Cars are an addictive drug that is killing the planet. The auto industry has succeeded in getting entire nations hooked. Now it's trying to push its poison on the rest of the world. In looking at the history of the automobile in America, car makers worked, conspired and used their influence to create a need for their products. If we are going to overcome our automobile addiction, we must curtail these pushers by not buying their products and by restricting their ability to promote and sell them at home and abroad. ∎

THE PRICE OF OIL

6 Associated Press, "Ford, Bridgestone Trade Tire Charges," New York Times on the Web, Sept. 12, 2000.
7 Glen Martin, "Valdez Spill Leaves Bitter Residue," San Francisco Chronicle, March 24, 1999, p. A1.
8 Paul Lewis, "Blood and Oil: A Special Report," New York Times, March 13, 1996, p. A1.

9 Kurt Eichenwald, "Texaco Executives, On Tape, Discussed Impending Bias Suit," New York Times, Nov. 4, 1996, p. A1; Kurt Eichenwald, "First Casualties in Scandal at Texaco," New York Times, Nov. 7, 1996, p. D1.

A CONSUMER

A CONSUMER (THE BIGGER VIEW)

"The automobile manu-
facturers, in general, have
no moral sense and no
sense of responsibility—no
ethics. They simply will do
anything if they think there
are enough stupid people
around to buy it."

*- Tom and Ray Magliozzi,
Cartalk Show no. 16,
National Public Radio*

"It is clear that the sales success of the automotive industry is not simply due to the willingness of customers to buy, but also to public policy that ignores needs for rapid transit and builds the highways and provides other services that make possible the growth of the automotive subeconomy. It is also clear that the manufacturers are increasingly relying upon and encouraging a demand for automobiles which has little to do with a demand for transportation."

- Ralph Nader, "Unsafe At Any Speed: The Designed-In Dangers of the American Automobile," 1965

Q: WHERE CAN A SOCIALLY CONSCIOUS PERSON BUY GAS?

A: NOWHERE, TIME TO STOP DRIVING!

"Shell operations still impossible unless ruthless military operations are undertaken for smooth economic activities to commence."

*- Nigerian military officer Paul Okuntimo,
in a 1998 confidential note to the Nigerian government*

**"We want to create a world called Select,
a world which revolves around shopping and driving."**

*- a Shell spokesperson in Nottingham, when announcing 400 new garages
in 1998 and a greater collaboration with Burger King*

"In its first 'corporate citizenship report' issued at the company's annual shareholders' meeting, Ford admitted sport utility vehicles contributed more than cars to global warming, emitted more smog-causing pollution and endangered other motorists. But the automaker said it would keep building them because they provide much needed profit. 'If we didn't provide that vehicle, someone else would...,' said William Clay Ford Jr., the company's chairman."

- Keith Bradsher, New York Times, May 12, 2000

THEY CAME FROM THE PLANET WALL STREET IN A HOSTILE BID TO TAKE OVER THE WORLD

INVASION OF THE CORPORATRONS

ARE Y-YOU THEIR L-LEADER?

NO, I'M HIS ATTORNEY, **TAKE ME TO YOUR ASSETS!**

ATM

THE CORPORATRONS HAD USED UP ALL THEIR RESOURCES...

...ON INDUSTRIAL GARBAGE DUMPS OF CARS, TELEVISIONS AND PLASTIC JUNK.

WHERE'S MY HAIR DRYER?

THEY NEEDED RAW MATERIALS (AND NEW CONSUMERS) TO MAKE MORE CRAP.

WE'RE OUT OF WATER, MINERALS, OIL, AIR AND ...SODA!

UH-OH... NO DIET PEPSI!?

SO THEY DECIDED TO **INVADE** THE **EARTH!**

IT HAS ENORMOUS MARKETING POTENTIAL

EARTH

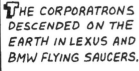 THE CORPORATRONS DESCENDED ON THE EARTH IN LEXUS AND BMW FLYING SAUCERS.

 C.F.O. TO C.E.O., "THE ATTORNEYS HAVE LANDED!"

USING TELEVISIONS WITH ENDLESS ADVERTISING AND BAD PROGRAMMING, THEY HYPNOTIZED EVERYONE...

 I MUST SPEND MONEY TO ENJOY MYSELF

BUY PEPSI

... AND, THUS, ENSLAVED THE EARTH'S POPULATION IN DEMEANING JOBS.

 WILL THAT BE CASH OR CHARGE?

REGISTER #3

HAVING GOTTEN THE EARTHLINGS HOOKED ON USELESS CONSUMER GOODS,

 I LOVE MY NEW HAND--HELD, COMPUTERIZED SALAD SPINNER!

CHECK OUT MY ELECTRIC BREAD-KNIFE.

ANIMALS, MINERALS, PLANTS, SOIL, AIR AND WATER WERE ALL NEEDED BACK HOME FOR MANUFACTURING.

THE CORPORATRONS BEGAN EXTRACTING EARTH'S NATURAL RESOURCES.

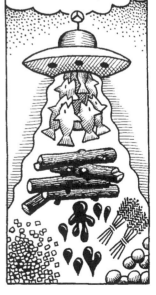

67

THE CORPORATRONS LOADED ALL THE EARTH'S RESOURCES INTO THEIR FLYING SAUCERS AND PREPARED TO TAKE OFF...

(... LEAVING THE EARTH AN OVERFISHED, DEFORESTED AND POLLUTED WASTELAND)

... BUT THEIR FLYING SAUCERS **WOULDN'T START!**

CLICK!
CLICK!

VICTIMS OF THEIR OWN LACK OF CONSUMER PROTECTION

OIL

SUDDENLY, THEY REALIZED **THEY WERE TRAPPED ON EARTH** WITH EVERYONE ELSE!

OIL

WILL THEY EVER **LEARN** TO CARE FOR THE PLANET AND SUSTAINABLY USE ITS RESOURCES??

NAHHHH!

WE COULD ALWAYS **SELL** THIS STUFF...

THE END!

A. SINGER

CARpe DIEM

(AN 'OUT-OF-CAR' EXPERIENCE)

"The dreams are aging in our day: boredom with motorization is widespread, and contrary images are becoming evident; the preference for bicycles is growing, and the idea of an unhurried society finds fertile soil on which to fall."

- Wolfgang Sachs, "For Love of the Automobile," 1984

Fortunately there is hope. Alternatives to a car-based society are just waiting to be seized. They come in three main forms: personal choices, improvements in public transportation, and fundamental changes in urban design. Let's start with the easiest one, the personal.

For me, the first step in stopping car culture is to STOP DRIVING! For many car owners (even ones who consider themselves to be "environmentalists") this seems like a radical and impossible step, but it's not as hard as it sounds. In my 38 years, I have never owned a car, and I can honestly say it's not a hardship. It just requires some planning when deciding where to live and where to work. You need to situate yourself in an urban or dense suburban area, with bus or transit lines, preferably within walking or biking distance from your job and basic services (groceries, bank, post office, etc.). In fact, not owning a car has many benefits. To begin with, you save an average of US$3,100 per year that you'd have to spend to own and maintain a car.

By living near your job or working near your home, you can save hundreds of hours of driving each year, giving yourself more free time to do other things (like draw cartoons). From having to walk or bike a little more, you stay in better shape and learn to be more efficient with your trips away from the house. Finally, by using public transit, you become a better advocate for it since you know more exactly how it works and how it could be improved.

When I absolutely need a car, I rent or borrow one. The thousands of dollars you save each year can buy a lot of car rentals. In Europe, Canada and even the U.S., people also form "car clubs," where several people share the costs and use of a single car. There are also "car-sharing organizations," where larger groups share several cars.

As we begin to stop driving, the next step is building more and better public transit. As I mentioned earlier, the problems of moving thousands of commuters into and out of city centers every day are unmanageable by highway lanes whose peak capacity is just 1,500 cars per hour. A single track of transit, however, can carry between 40,000 and 50,000 people per hour and it can bring them in without their cars...so they won't require parking![1] Moreover, a transit line is spatially less destructive of the human and wildlife environments through which it passes. Even buses are a vast improvement over cars. A single bus has the capacity of 25 to 50 cars. If one slightly wider lane is reserved for buses on an expressway, between 400 and 800 buses can use that lane in an hour. The capacity of that lane becomes 20,000 people per hour instead of the 4,500 maximum that is possible with cars.[2] But don't let highway builders convince you to add new bus or High Occupancy Vehicle lanes. Instead, convert existing lanes into HOV lanes or transit right-of-ways. In general, public transportation projects should take road space away from cars. Otherwise, alternatives would just be offered on top of the car-based system rather than changing it fundamentally.[3] This way, a former four-lane boulevard can provide for a two-way light-rail line, while reducing car lanes (and maximum car traffic) by half.

Building better public transit systems will require structural changes in government. By itself, a highway authority or department tries to do one thing: build highways! By integrating highway and transit authorities into one single department, however, the combined authority is forced to take a more balanced approach. Gas tax revenues and tolls from highways can be used to fund trains, and the combined department can give more objective advice to legislatures. New York did this in the late 1960s, creating the MTA, and saved its transit systems from total annihilation. Once we integrate transportation departments, we need to make them more publicly accountable and fill their boards with people opposed to new roads and sympathetic to public transit.

Finally, there needs to be fundamental changes in urban design. To make public transit work you need "mass"—a certain density of people. A walking community and public transit are interdependent. To get an hourly bus in a residential district, you need at least four houses per acre. In a commercial district, you need at least five million square feet of retail space. Light rail on surface tracks requires at least nine homes per acre or 20 million square feet of retail space.[4] To get this kind of density you need to "infill" suburbs, adding houses and allowing three- to four-unit apartment buildings, and you need to create small town centers, transit hubs or "TODs" (Transit-Oriented Developments). To do this you need good zoning laws.

Zoning has a tremendous impact on transit. Besides increasing population density, mixed-use zoning can allow jobs and retail space to be situated near housing, putting jobs and basic services within walking distance of homes and reducing the need for people to travel. Conversely, in crowded cities, good zoning laws ensure that development does not outpace the transit (and other service) infrastructures. Needless to say, incredibly important decisions are made by zoning boards. We need to fill zoning boards with people who will enact laws that limit sprawl, and promote higher density, walkability

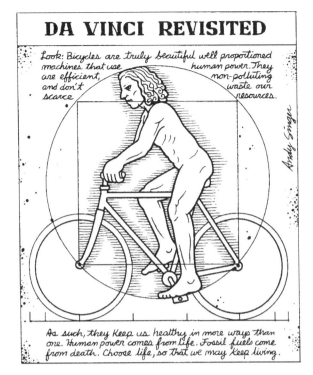

DA VINCI REVISITED

Look: Bicycles are truly beautiful well proportioned machines. that use human power. They are efficient, non-polluting and don't waste our scarce resources.

As such, they keep us healthy in more ways than one. Human power comes from life. Fossil fuels come from death. Choose life, so that we may keep living.

Andy Singer

"Man on a bicycle can go three or four times faster than the pedestrian, but uses five times less energy in the process...The bicycle is the perfect transducer to match man's metabolic energy to the impedance of locomotion."

- Ivan Illich, "Energy and Equity," 1973

and public transit. On a regional and national level, urban growth boundaries, road pricing and a freeze on road building should be instituted to reduce driving and combat sprawl. Gas taxes should also be raised to reflect the true costs of driving (to include the so-called "externalities").

Major efforts should be made to make cities more livable. These should include noise ordinances that ban car alarms, limit late-night emergency sirens and restrict hours for construction. Small parks and other green spaces should be planned and built. At the neighborhood level, bike lanes, traffic calming and "street reclaiming"[5] should be instituted wherever possible. That is, street space should be reclaimed psychologically and physically from traffic. A parking lot can be transformed into a playground, garden or community space. Cars can be slowed down or eliminated using signal lights, stop signs, humps, bumps, barriers or sidewalk "bulb-outs." Traffic calming reduces noise, lessens the danger of cars to pedestrians, and builds community. More city streets should be made car-free and, where possible, private cars should be banned from city centers entirely.

Some of this can be done easily by small groups of people, but to do it all will require sustained pressure on officials and politicians at all levels. Creating on-line news groups (like Bay Area Transit) around local and national transportation issues is a great way of informing and mobilizing people to call legislators, write editorials and attend public hearings. Holding monthly "Critical Mass" bike rides or pedestrian/

IT'S THE URBAN SAFETY CYCLE

REVOLVING LIGHTS FOR BETTER VISIBILITY

PADS

AIR BAGS

WARD FENNER + SLOAN

30mm CANNON

ATTORNEY

DOG-PROOF LEG GUARDS

TITANIUM ALLOY CRUSH-PROOF AUTO-SAFETY CAGE

TM A.B. SINGER

HEAVY WHEELS + SUSPENSION FOR EVEN **DEEP** POTHOLES

transit rider gatherings is also a great way to educate people about the issues. Stopping car culture will require lawyers and lawsuits to stop roads from being built and to block further suburban development.

In this and all areas, knowledge of existing laws and history is helpful. There is a wealth of resources and information devoted to these subjects. The books, web sites and organizations listed at the end of this book are but a small sampling.

Most of the ideas in this chapter have been around for a long time. All they require is the collective will to make them happen. ■

1 Robert A. Caro, The Power Broker, (New York, Vintage Books, 1974), p. 901.

2 Ibid, p. 945.

3 Randy Ghent, "Thoughts on Induced Traffic and Public Space," in Car Busters no. 10, p. 25.

4 Boris S. Pushkarev and Jeffrey M. Zupan, Public Transport and Land Use Policy, (Bloomington, IN: Indiana University Press, 1977), pp. 185-188.

5 David Engwicht, Street Reclaiming: Creating Livable Streets and Vibrant Communities, (Sydney, NSW: Pluto Press Australia, 1999; distributed in North America by New Society Publishers).

WE'VE APPEASED NON-SMOKERS...
NOW, LET'S APPEASE NON-DRIVERS!!
DIVIDE CITIES INTO TWO SECTIONS:
DRIVING AND NON-DRIVING

"Those who see for the future a tightly interwoven national and international society cannot give up speed and penetrability. Those, however, who hope for an economy that is locally denser and internationally less enmeshed can afford prudence and insist on the integrity of the near...
"The right to visit a distant place now retreats behind the right to recapture one's own place; the habitability of the immediate vicinity will no longer be sacrificed to the accessibility of distant locales."

- Wolfgang Sachs, "For the Love of the Automobile," 1984

EVOLUTION

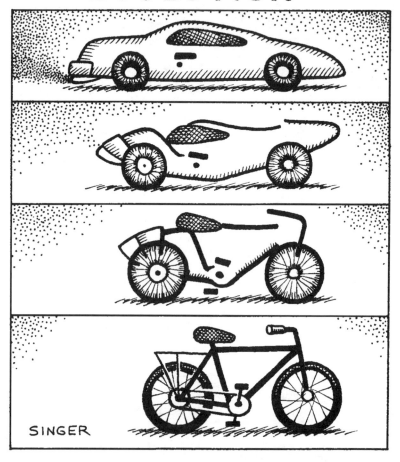

SINGER

"Eighteen bikes can be parked in the space of one car, thirty of them can move along in the space devoured by a single automobile. It takes two lanes of a given size to move 40,000 people across a bridge in one hour by using modern trains, four to move them by buses, twelve to move them in their cars and only one lane for them to pedal across on bicycles."

- Ivan Illich, "Energy and Equity," 1973

"The automobiles required to transport the equivalent of one trainload of commuters use about four acres of parking space."

- Robert Caro, "The Power Broker," 1974

(ANOTHER SET OF EARDRUMS SAVED BY *CAR-ALARM MAN!*)

"Participatory democracy demands low-energy technology, and free people must travel the road to productive social relations at the speed of a bicycle."

- Ivan Illich, "Energy and Equity," 1973

A NONPOLLUTING WEDDING PROCESSION

"When I see an adult on a bicycle, I do not despair
for the future of the human race."

- H.G. Wells, 1920s

"Norway recently banned the construction of large shopping centers outside city center areas for five years in a bid to reduce automobile pollution and revive ailing downtowns. 'The government wants to revitalize and strengthen the downtowns of cities and towns as the most important gathering point for people, businesses and cultural activities,' Minister of the Environment Guro Fjellander said in announcing the decision."

- Associated Press, January 1999

**"Nothing we can do with mass transit can match
the effect of lessening the need for people to travel."**

*- Sam Smith, "Saving Our Cities from the Experts,"
in "City Kids/City Teachers," 1996*

"The bicycle offers the gains of advanced technology without threatening the environment. It stands not only for undamaged nature but also for unbroken autonomy. To attack the pedals may be strenuous over the short run, but it is an expression of trust in one's own powers, for with the bicycle everything depends on the self. Those who wish to control their own lives and move beyond existence as mere clients and consumers—those people ride a bike."

- Wolfgang Sachs, "For Love of the Automobile," 1984

"We can see every day more and more cyclists in Warsaw. One Danish company has started delivering letters and packages by bike. This has proved successful because cyclists don't have to wait in traffic jams. A few other companies have started using bikes, too, for sending messages, delivering pizzas, etc. 'Ordinary' people have been inspired by these couriers, and there are crowds of cyclists now—crowds by Warsaw standards—which don't yet compare to The Netherlands at all, not yet."

- Zuzanna Iskierka, Warsaw, Poland, 1998

TRAFFIC SLAYER

84

CAR WARS
(THE EMPOWERED STRIKE BACK)

BY RANDY GHENT

"Two fronts have formed in the struggle: the will of the people and the will of the government. The people do not want the automobile; the government, or a part of it, wants to admit it under whatever conditions necessary."

- Felici Maissen, "Der Kampf um das Automobil in Graubünden 1900-1925," 1968

It's clear. A growing movement has formed to liberate the world's cities from the car, a growing movement making itself heard louder and louder across international boundaries and language barriers.

And it's not too late for you to join in. Luckily, there are campaigns to fit with every sensibility, whether you're most comfortable educating children, meeting with city planners, doing research, writing press releases, or spending your summer at a blockade camp. It's all important work. There are also lots of creative action ideas that can be carried out by a very small group of people (or just one person). This extra chapter (you get seven chapters for the price of six!) provides a sampler to get your brain stimulated and your heart jumping:

• In New York City, a group called Right of Way has called attention to what they call "car violence" by painting memorials to car victims. Each memorial is a life-size body outline, with the victim's name and the date he or she was "KILLED BY AUTOMOBILE" painted in a crosswalk or sidewalk.

• When Madrid's mayor proposed a network of 140 kilometers of underground highways, the group Ecologistas en Acción presented the city leaders with a life-size "genetically modified creature," half-human and half mole, designed to survive in the new urban habitat. Homo Madritensis Futuribilis appeared frequently at tunnel inaugurations and peppered the mayor's re-election campaign with shows of "gratitude" for such excavating enthusiasm. ➤

- In San Francisco, multiple pie throwers of the mysterious Biotic Baking Brigade successfully tossed three pies at the face of Chevron oil company CEO Kenneth Derr before disappearing on bicycles without a trace. BBB Agent 3.14 launched the first strike after saying to Derr, "Do people really kill Nigerians for oil? People Do," in reference to Chevron's "People Do" ad campaign.

- Many groups have held public "potluck" meals to build community, but very few have done it in the middle of the street. Mobil Ohne Auto (Mobile Without Cars) in Münster, Germany, has organized several "breakfast actions," cordoning off roadside parking spaces for a communal breakfast. "We're taking back our living space," said one breakfaster. "There's enough parking space, but too little space for people in this town."

- Tooker Gomberg and Angela Bischoff were simply ambling along St. Denis, one of Montreal's great strolling streets, when they spotted a couch awaiting the garbage truck. They settled into the sofa, soaked up some rays, read the paper, and unexpectedly the sofa became a tool for liberating a small chunk of asphalt from the cars. Thousands of passersby smiled; many burst out laughing. Photographers snapped. Parents chuckled and elbowed their kids to look. One woman joined in and heckled the crowd: "Bring out your furniture. We need a kitchen table." The spontaneous action lasted two hours before a couple sour police officers slapped Gomberg and Bischoff with two "couch in the street" fines.

- A group of English women in their '80s from a local pedestrians' association are rumored to have started what's now called "car bouncing." When confronted with a car parked on the sidewalk blocking their path, they would simply surround the car and "bounce" it back into the street.

- At an action camp against Germany's A17 highway, activists erected giant picture frames beside the highway, looking like roadside billboards. Except they had hollow centers, "framing" the threatened landscape, and quoting Goëthe: "Why wander in the vastness; see the Good lies so near."

- The infamous "manif spaciale" (spacial demonstration) developed by the Montreal group Le Monde à Bicyclette is simply a group of cyclists riding around with giant "space frames" attached to their bikes, making them take up the same amount of space as a car. First there's the humor of it—a bicycle taking up so much space is kind of ridiculous. And that is precisely the point: why take up so much space to move one person around? How wasteful! And you can pedal along at your own leisurely pace, without worrying about flying car doors, having to ride right next to the curb, or speeding cars

MOSES PARTS TRAFFIC

Michael Hartmann of Munich earned near-celebrity status across Germany for walking over cars blocking the sidewalk, and achieving a German Supreme Court decision that permits pedestrians to do so. Since then he's adopted a newer tactic: "Street walking" involves calmly and confidently walking in a straight line toward one's destination—often diagonally across a street—regardless of whether there's an intersection, crosswalk, red light, or a semi-truck speeding toward you. Hartmann claims that street lights were originally just for cars—from 1923 to 1927 in Paris, anyway—and that pedestrians could cross anywhere.

G.M.'s LAST STAND

Critical Mass bicycle rides have occurred in over 230 cities around the world, bring together a mass of up to several thousand cyclists during the evening rush hour. There are no real organisers; people just show up each month and organically decide when the ride will begin. They make the point, "We're not blocking traffic, we *are* traffic," since cyclists—on every other day of the month—don't get their fair share of public roads. The largest rides occur in London, Sydney, Melbourne and San Francisco.

coming close to you (since drivers are afraid of marring their paint jobs).

• Activists with the group Maloka in Dijon, France, have taken to building cardboard cars with wooden frames, shopping cart wheels, and grimacing faces. The activists paint them with slogans such as "I pollute, make my driver aggressive and never will I let you live until 2012!" Then they ride them around Fred Flintstone-like to animate their demonstrations, at least until people spitting fire from their mouths burn them in a ritual sacrifice to the god of public space.

• Bike enthusiasts in San Francisco combined the above two ideas into a counter protest of a counter protest. When 15 car enthusiasts organized a "Car Critical Mass" to protest what they saw as the city government's bias against drivers, the car drivers found themselves outnumbered by a good-natured group who showed up driving "sport-utility bicycles."

• After the city government in Warsaw, Poland, stalled the building of a bike lane for two years, activists with the Green Federation painted a 600-yard-long bike lane themselves without permission, with 150 participants of a "Critical Mass" bicycle demonstration joining in. They demanded the city build more bike lanes, or such actions would be repeated every month.

CAR FIGHTING
(...OR "THE RUNNING OF THE CARS")

• City Repair, in Portland, Oregon, transforms intersections into lively public squares. One of them, "Share-It Square," features a community bulletin board, public benches, a produce station (where people can get, give away or exchange food freely), an arts and crafts station (where passers-by can take or donate handmade items), and what one newspaper called "a hanging collection of mugs and a thermos called the T-station," which provides free hot tea 24 hours a day. Organic gardens grow in sidewalk planter strips, and a brightly painted giant mandala fills the road surface of the entire intersection, symbolizing the new sense of community.

• Since 1995, "Reclaim the Streets" street parties have broken out all over the world. Everyone's invited, but only a few know the location. Two old cars collide, and their actor-drivers pretend to be irate as they proceed to smash up each other's cars in the middle of a busy intersection. Meanwhile, party-goers are led to the scene from a designated meeting point and the party begins. Out comes a sandbox, a band and stage, juggling balls, face paints, living room furniture—anything to recreate the public space that has been lost to the private space of moving metal boxes (cars). The largest party of 1996 saw 8,000 people reclaim, redecorate and plant trees in a London motorway.

• Knowing full well that their city council would never support World Carfree Day, activists in Adelaide, Australia, decided to announce the event themselves. They printed up 1,000 posters and 5,000 flyers announcing the center of Adelaide would be closed to cars, placing official governmental logos at the bottom. The State Minister of Transport "really freaked out" when handed a leaflet. The South Australia government and the Adelaide City Council felt compelled to issue a press release to unveil the hoax. Consequently it received two days of television, radio and print coverage before the "event." One of the activists wrote: "Could it have been my imagination or did there really seem to be fewer cars in the city that day? I know of at least five people who didn't drive into town because they believed the posters and didn't see the media announcing the hoax."

As these examples have shown, imagination can be the antidote to boring predictability. It can inspire participants as well as the public, and keep your targets on their toes. Of course the point is not to emulate the actions of others, but to use them as inspiration for something new that fits your local culture and circumstances. So go on then, what are you waiting for? ∎

CAR NET D'ADRESSES

(THAT'S FRENCH FOR 'ADDRESS BOOK')

ACCESS - EUROCITIES FOR A NEW MOBILITY CULTURE
A network of European cities promoting environmentally friendlier modes of transport. A platform for the exchange of experience, information and good practice.
c/o Eurocities
18 Square de Meeus
1050 Brussels, Belgium
tel: +(32) 2-552-08-83
fax: +(32) 2-552-08-89
e-mail: access@eurocities.be
web: www.access-eurocities.org

ADVOCACY FOR RESPECT FOR CYCLISTS (ARC)
An active, creative fun-loving Toronto bike activist group.
761 Queen St. W., Suite 101
Toronto, Ont. M6J 1G1, Canada
tel: +1(416) 604-5171
e-mail: arc@respect.to
web: www.respect.to

AMERICA WALKS
A national coalition of local advocacy groups promoting walkable communities, assisting community pedestrian groups and educating the public.
Old City Hall
45 School St., 2nd Floor
Boston, MA 02108, USA
tel: +1(617) 367-1170
fax: +1(617) 367-9285
e-mail: info@americawalks.org
web: www.americawalks.org

AUTOFREI LEBEN!
A German carfree network. A voice for people who live or want to live carfree. Organizes activities to publicize and promote carfree living.
Koppenplatz 12
D-10115 Berlin-Mitte, Germany
tel: +(49) 30-2759-4244
e-mail: verein@autofrei.de
web: www.autofrei.de

BICYCLE TRANSPORTATION ALLIANCE (BTA)
Portland, Oregon's cycling advocates, "creating safe, sane and sustainable communities, one bike at a time."
P.O. Box 9072
Portland, OR 97207, USA
tel: +1(503) 226-0676
fax: +1(503) 226-0498
e-mail: info@bta4bikes.org
web: www.bta4bikes.org

BIKES AT WORK, INC.
Operates a pedal-powered collection and delivery service and a pedicab. Builds and sells bike trailers.
129 Washington Avenue
Ames, IA 50010, USA
tel: +1(515) 233-6120
web: www.bikesatwork.com

BIKES NOT BOMBS
Operates a Bicycle Recycling and Youth Training Center to promote environmental education, meaningful employment, and safe, sustainable communities.
59 Armory Street
Roxbury, MA 02119, USA
tel: +1(617) 442-0004
e-mail: mail@bikesnotbombs.org
web: www.bikesnotbombs.org

CAR BUSTERS MAGAZINE
The quarterly magazine of the global carfree movement.
Kratka 26, 100 00 Prague 10
Czech Republic
tel: +(420) 274-810-849
fax: +(420) 274-772-017
e-mail: info@carbusters.org
web: www.carbusters.org

CARFREE.COM
Images and information on carfree city design by J.H. Crawford, the author of "Carfree Cities." Also features an on-line quarterly

Carfree Times newsletter.
e-mail: mail@carfree.com
web: www.carfree.com

CARSHARING.NET
Provides contact information and links to carsharing programs worldwide, and shows you how to set up your own carshare program.

CENTER FOR APPROPRIATE TRANSPORT
Cycling and pedestrian advocacy group that builds work bikes, recumbents and trailers; provides youth bike education and training.
455 West 1st Avenue
Eugene, OR 97401, USA
tel: +1(541) 344-1197
fax: +1(541) 686-1015
e-mail: cat@efn.org
web: www.efn.org/~cat

CHICAGOLAND BICYCLE FEDERATION
A vigorous bike advocacy group, promoting cycling safety, education and facilities improvements in the Chicago region.
650 S. Clark Street, #300
Chicago, IL 60605, USA
tel: +1(312) 42-PEDAL
fax: +1(312) 427-4907
e-mail: cbf@biketraffic.org
web: www.biketraffic.org

CITY REPAIR
An organized group action that educates and inspires communities and individuals to creatively transform the places where they live. They facilitate artistic and ecologically orientated placemaking.
PO Box 42615
Portland, OR 97242, USA
tel: +1(503) 235-8946
tel: +1(503) 235-1046
e-mail: thecircle@cityrepair.org
web: www.cityrepair.org

CONGRESS FOR THE NEW URBANISM

The New Urbanism movement seeks to reform all aspects of real estate development and promote denser walkable communities with a mix of jobs and housing.
140 S. Dearborn St., Suite 310
Chicago, IL 60603
tel: +1(312) 551-7300
fax: +1(312) 346-3323
e-mail: cnuinfo@cnu.org
web: www.cnu.org

CONSERVATION LAW FOUNDATION

A large New England environmental advocacy organization. Features several excellent publications on alternative transport and traffic calming, free via their website. These include: "Take Back Your Streets: How to Protect Communities from Asphalt and Traffic."
62 Summer Street
Boston, MA 02110-1016, USA
tel: +1(617) 350-0990
fax: +1(617) 350-4030
web: www.clf.org

CRITICAL-MASS.ORG AND CRITICALMASSRIDES.INFO

Critical Mass bike rides are monthly celebrations in which cyclists ride together in one big group and take back the streets. See these websites to find your nearest ride, or start your own!

DETOUR'S URBANSOURCE

On-line source for books and resources on transportation and urban ecology; free catalogue.
850 Coxwell Ave., 2nd Floor
Toronto, Ont. M4C 5R1, Canada
tel: +1(416) 338-5087
fax: +1(416) 392-0071
info@detourpublications.com
www.detourpublications.com

ECOPLAN INTERNATIONAL

Think tank on sustainability and urban issues; host organization for The Commons, an internet-based forum with discussions on carfree days, car sharing and more.
La Frene, 8/10 Rue Joseph Bara
F-75006 Paris, France
tel: +(33) 1-43-26-13-23
fax: +(33) 1-44-41-63-41
e-mail: Eric.Britton@ecoplan.org
web: www.ecoplan.org

ENGWICHT COMMUNICATIONS

David Engwicht's books, videos and traffic reduction tools.
7 Fletcher Parade
Bardon, Qld 4065, Australia
tel: +(61) 7-33-66-77-46
e-mail: david@lesstraffic.com
web: www.lesstraffic.com

EUROPEAN FEDERATION FOR TRANSPORT AND ENVIRONMENT

Lobbying and advocacy for sustainable transport; maintains a network of member groups across Europe; publishes the free T&E Bulletin.
Boulevard de Waterloo 34
B-1000 Brussels, Belgium
tel: +(32) 2-502-9909
fax: +(32) 2-502-9908
e-mail: info@t-e.nu
web: www.t-e.nu

EUROPEAN CYCLISTS FEDERATION

A network of bicycle users' groups across Europe; E.U. lobbying; annual Velo City conferences; consultancy services; info source.
c/o ADFC, Grünenstrasse 120
28199 Bremen, Germany
tel: +(49) 421-346-29-39
fax: +(49) -346-29-50
e-mail: office@ecf.com
web: www.ecf.com

INSTITUTE FOR TRANSPORTATION & DEVELOPMENT POLICY

A leader in developing and implementing green transport policy in the developing world, as an alternative to the U.S. model. Innovative projects in nearly every corner of the world.
115 W. 30th St., Suite 1205
New York, NY 10001, USA
tel: +1(212) 629-8001
fax: +1(212) 629-8033
e-mail: mobility@itdp.org
web: www.itdp.org

INTERNATIONAL ASSOCIATION OF PUBLIC TRANSPORT

Provides information, research, and analysis on all aspects of public transport.
UITP Main Office
Rue Sainte-Marie 6
B-1080 Brussels, Belgium
tel: +(32) 2-673-61-00
fax: +(32) 2-660-10-72
e-mail: info@uitp.com
web: www.uitp.com

LEAGUE OF AMERICAN BICYCLISTS

National education, advocacy and lobby group; sponsors National Bike Month and Bike-to-Work Day; quarterly magazine; website links to state/local U.S. bike groups.
1612 K Street NW, Suite 800
Washington, DC 20006, USA
tel: +1(202) 822-1333
fax: +1(202) 822-1334
e-mail: bikeleague@bikeleague.org
web: www.bikeleague.org

NATIONAL ASSOCIATION OF RAILROAD PASSENGERS

Promotes intercity passenger rail service in the U.S. Offers fare discounts and info to train travelers.
900 2nd St., NE, Suite 308
Washington, DC 20002, USA
tel: +1(202) 408-8362
fax: +1(202) 408-8287
e-mail: narp@narprail.org
web: www.narprail.org

NATIONAL CENTER FOR BICYCLING AND WALKING

Supports the activities and initiatives of people working to make America a better place to walk and ride a bicycle. Website has some good practical on-line publications and resources for cycling and pedestrian advocates.
8120 Woodmont Ave, Suite 650
Bethesda, MD 20814, USA
tel: +1(301) 656-4220
fax: +1(301) 656-4225
e-mail: info@bikewalk.org
web: www.bikewalk.org

PEDALS FOR PROGRESS

Rescues bicycles destined for U.S. landfills and ships them to countries in the "third world."
P.O. Box 312
High Bridge, NJ 08829, USA
tel: +1(908) 638-4811
fax: +1(908) 638-4860
e-mail: globaloperations@p4p.org
p4p.offoce@earthlink.net
web: www.p4p.org

PROJECT FOR PUBLIC SPACES

Works with local groups and authorities to establish healthy public spaces, often by taking space away from car infrastructure.

continued next page ➤

153 Waverly Place, 4th Floor
New York, NY 10014, USA
tel: +1(212) 620-5660
fax: +1(212) 620-3821
e-mail: pps@pps.org
web: www.pps.org

PYATOK ARCHITECTS, INC.

Award-winning design firm, focusing on community planning, affordable housing and higher density mixed-use developments. Committed to participatory design processes.
1611 Telegraph Ave., Suite 200
Oakland, CA 94612, USA
tel: +1(510) 465-7010
e-mail: office@pyatok.com
web: www.pyatok.com

RAILS-TO-TRAILS CONSERVANCY

Works with local communities to convert abandoned railroad lines into public pathways for non-automotive transportation.
1100 17th Street NW, 10th Floor
Washington, DC 20036, USA
tel: +1(202) 331-9696
fax: +1(202) 331-9680
e-mail: railstrails@railtrails.org
web: www.railtrails.org

SAN FRANCISCO BICYCLE COALITION

Bicycle advocacy group "dedicated to making San Francisco the most bike-friendly city in the nation."
1095 Market St. #215
San Francisco, CA 94103, USA
tel: +1(415) 431-BIKE
e-mail: info@sfbike.org
web: www.sfbike.org

SIERRA CLUB CHALLENGE TO SPRAWL CAMPAIGN

Has reports, resources, facts and figures on-line about sprawl and how to stop it. "Promotes smart growth communities that increase transportation choices."
85 Second Street, Second Floor
San Francisco, CA 94105, USA
tel: +1(415) 977-5500
fax: +1(415) 977-5799
web: www.sierraclub.org/sprawl

SPRAWLWATCH.ORG

Makes the tools, techniques, and strategies developed to manage growth accessible to citizens, planners and officials. Collects, compiles, and disseminates information on the best practices.

SURFACE TRANSPORTATION POLICY PROJECT (STPP)

Large U.S. national lobby group that advocates for sustainable transportation. Publishes many useful reports and newsletters, most of which are available for free on its website.
1100 17th St., NW, 10th Floor
Washington, DC 20036
tel: +1(202) 466-2636
fax: +1(202) 466-2247
e-mail: stpp@transact.org
web: www.transact.org

TRAFFICCALMING.ORG

A website sponsored by Fehr & Peers Transportation Consultants. Features descriptions, photos and information on many of the more popular traffic calming measures used by traffic engineers.

TRANSPORTATION ALTERNATIVES

New York City's advocates for cyclists, pedestrians and sensible transportation. Publishes an excellent quarterly newsletter by the same name.
115 West 30th Street, Suite 1207
New York, NY 10001, USA
tel: +1(212) 629-8080
fax: +1(212) 629-8334
e-mail: info@transalt.org
web: www.transalt.org

UNION OF CONCERNED SCIENTISTS

Develops strategies to reduce the environmental, public health, and economic impacts of the U.S. transportation system. Its web site is a great source of info on auto emissions, air pollution and global warming.
2 Brattle Square
Cambridge, MA 02238, USA
tel: +1(617) 547-5552
fax: +1(617) 864-9405
e-mail: ucs@ucsusa.org
www.ucsusa.org/transportation/

VICTORIA TRANSPORT POLICY INSTITUTE

Independent research organization dedicated to developing innovative and practical tools for solving transportation problems. Provides a wide range of studies, guides and software, most available free on its website.

1250 Rudlin Street
Victoria, BC, V8V 3R7, Canada
tel: +1(250) 360-1560
e-mail: info@vtpi.org
web: www.vtpi.org

WALKABLE COMMUNITIES, INC.

Organized to help communities become more walkable and pedestrian friendly. Offers presentations, walkable audits, training courses, workshops, and more. Has many on-line resources, as well as publications, video tapes, slide sets and photo CDs to assist in community education.
320 South Main Street
High Springs, FL 32643, USA
tel: +1(386) 454-3304
e-mail: walkable@aol.com
web: www.walkable.org

WILDLANDS CENTER FOR PREVENTING ROADS

Works to protect and restore wildland ecosystems by preventing and removing roads and limiting motorized recreation on public land. Clearinghouse on wilderness road impacts and road-fighting strategies. Publishes Road RIPorter.
P.O. Box 7516
Missoula, MT 59807, USA
tel: +1(406) 543-9551
wildlandsCPR@wildlandscpr.org
web: www.wildlandscpr.org

WORLD CARFREE NETWORK

The hub of the global carfree movement, with member organizations around the world and many international projects.
Kratka 26
100 00 Prague 10
Czech Republic
tel: +(420) 274-810-849
fax: +(420) 274-772-017
e-mail: info@worldcarfree.net
web: www.worldcarfree.net

WORLD TRANSPORT POLICY AND PRACTICE JOURNAL

Quarterly academic journal specializing in innovative sustainable transport research worldwide.
John Whitelegg, Eco-logica Ltd.
53 Derwent Road
Lancaster LA1 3ES, U.K.
tel: +(44) 1524-63175
e-mail: pascaldesmond@eircom.net
web: www.eco-logica.co.uk/
WTPPhome.html

SELECTED BIBLIOGRAPHY

ALVORD, KATIE. Divorce Your Car: Ending the Love Affair with the Automobile. Gabriola Island, BC, Canada: New Society Publishers, 2000. An excellent and thorough analysis of the impact of cars on society and the environment. It investigates ways to stop driving and features a great list of organizations and resources.

BROWER, MICHAEL AND WARREN LEON. The Consumers Guide to Effective Environmental Choices: Practical Advice from the Union of Concerned Scientists. New York: Three Rivers Press, 1999. Looks at the environmental impact of different consumer choices. It singles out motor vehicles as one of the leading causes of environmental destruction.

CALTHORPE, PETER. The Next American Metropolis: Ecology, Community and the American Dream. New York: Princeton Architectural Press, 1993. An urban and regional planning manual for creating Transit Oriented Developments (TODs). It contains a good overview of the problems of sprawl, and presents case studies of actual regional plans, designed to reduce sprawl and enhance biking and walkability.

CARO, ROBERT. The Power Broker: Robert Moses and the Fall of New York. New York: Vintage Books, 1974. A Pulitzer Prize winning biography that gives an unparalleled look into the inner workings of a city and state highway authority. The book examines the political and economic power bases of highway agencies, how they wield that power and efforts (both successful and unsuccessful) to fight them.

DOWNS, ANTHONY. Stuck in Traffic: Coping with Peak-Hour Traffic Congestion. Washington, DC: The Brookings Institution, 1992. This book gives a detailed analysis of Traffic Congestion and, one by one, looks at all of the various proposed solutions. Its idea of "100 small cuts" is excellent. Alas, it does not consider larger environmental implications of proposed solutions. As such, it is only marginally useful.

GODDARD, STEPHEN. Getting There: The Epic Struggle Between Road and Rail in the American Century. New York: Basic Books, 1994. A historical analysis of why automobiles succeeded and American passenger rail and public transportation failed.

ILLICH, IVAN. Energy and Equity. London: Calder and Boyars Ltd., 1974. One of the most creative, thoughtful essays you will ever read—a bicycling and pedestrian manifesto. It considers the failings of modern transport and the relationship between a society's energy use and its level of social equity. (Available free in several languages as a text file from the Car Busters web site: <www.carbusters.ecn.cz>.)

KAY, JANE HOLTZ. Asphalt Nation: How the Automobile Took Over America and How We Can Take It Back. Berkeley, California: University of California Press, 1997. An excellent and thorough analysis of the history and impact of cars in the U.S., with particular focus on the way they have impacted architectural and urban space.

KITMAN, JAMIE LINCOLN. "The Secret History of Lead." The Nation 270 (March 20, 2000): 11-44. A thoroughly researched and well-written history of the collusion between General Motors, Standard Oil and Du Pont to make and market leaded gasoline—a deadly poison still sold all over the world. (Available free as a text file from the Car Busters web site: <www.carbusters.ecn.cz>.)

PUSHKAREV, BORIS S. AND JEFFREY ZUPAN. Public Transportation and Land Use Policy. Bloomington, Indiana: Indiana University Press, 1977. Based on studies prepared for the New York Tri-State Regional Planning Commission, this book considers what conditions of population density, fare price, frequency and travel time will enable different forms of public transport to be successful. It is fairly technical but features a brief, extremely interesting history of urban density, from ancient Egypt to the present day.

SACHS, WOLFGANG. For the Love of the Automobile. Berkeley, California: University of California Press, 1992. An English translation of the 1984 German original. It traces the history of the car in Germany (where it was invented) and looks at the social, philosophical and cultural implications of cars, car advertising and road construction.

CAR FREE GUIDE

(BOOKS FROM WORLD CARFREE NETWORK)

ASPHALT NATION
HOW THE AUTOMOBILE TOOK OVER AMERICA
AND HOW WE CAN TAKE IT BACK
JANE HOLTZ KAY, 1998, 440 PAGES

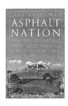

Asphalt Nation *is a powerful examination of how the automobile has ravaged America's cities and landscape over the past 100 years, together with a compelling strategy for reversing our automobile dependency. Demonstrating that there are economic, political, architectural, and personal solutions, Kay shows that radical change is entirely possible.*

CAR BUSTERS GRAPHICS BOOK
CAR BUSTERS, 1999, 44 PAGES

Our graphics book brings together the best graphics on file at Car Busters, from the artists you see in the magazine. Includes info on how to produce attractive posters, etc. The graphics can be reproduced freely (for non-profit purposes) by local groups for leaflets, posters, newsletters, etc.

CARFREE CITIES
J.H. CRAWFORD, 2000, 324 PAGES, HARD COVER

An unapologetic argument for car-free cities, the book works from the position that the car-free city is the cornerstone of sustainable development, and outlines a city structure carefully designed to maximise quality of life worldwide. It gives practical suggestions for implementing the reference design in existing cities, and much more.

CRITICAL MASS

BICYCLING'S DEFIANT CELEBRATION
CHRIS CARLSSON, ED., 2002, 256 PGS.

A pushy and irreverent collection of inkworthy social critique and optimistic celebration. Four dozen contributors document, define and drive home the beauty of a quiet ride with a thousand friends, the anarchy of grassroots inspiration, and the melodrama of media coverage.

CUTTING YOUR CAR USE
SAVE MONEY, BE HEALTHY, BE GREEN!
ANNA SEMLYEN, 2003, 96 PAGES

Britain's first personal traffic reduction guide. Packed with constructive, easy-to-follow, best-practice advice. For anyone who wants to cut their car use, or give up their car completely. A North American version (US/Canada) is coming in 2006, from New Society Publishers.

DIVORCE YOUR CAR
ENDING THE LOVE AFFAIR WITH THE AUTOMOBILE
KATIE ALVORD, 2000, 320 PAGES

Divorce Your Car! *speaks to individuals, encouraging readers to change their own driving behavior without waiting for broader social change, stressing that individual action can drive social change. From commuters crazed by congestion to soccer moms sick of chauffeuring,* Divorce Your Car! *provides all the reasons not to drive and the many carfree alternatives.*

EF! DIRECT ACTION MANUAL
DAM COLLECTIVE, 1998, 152 PAGES

Edited by a former Earth First! Journal co-editor, this is an almost comprehensive guide to direct action tactics developed around the world. Lots of useful diagrams and illustrations. A must-have for any direct action campaign.

THE END OF THE ROAD
FROM WORLD CAR CRISIS
TO SUSTAINABLE TRANSPORTATION
WOLFGANG ZUCKERMANN, 1991, 300 PP.

There are half a billion cars on the planet, and this is one of the earliest books to take a long, hard look at the contrast between the image and the reality of this fact. Zuckermann offers 33 "ways out" of our car dependence, including pedestrianisation, traffic calming, alternative transportation and rearranging our lives.

FAMILY MOUSE BEHIND THE WHEEL
WOLFGANG ZUCKERMANN, 1992

This colorful illustrated book teaches children the problems of car culture through the eyes of a family of anthropomorphized forest mice, who decide to buy a car, build a road into their previously intact forest, and eventually, create an urban hell. An eye-opener complete with the obligatory moralistic message.

FOR LOVE OF THE AUTOMOBILE
LOOKING BACK INTO THE HISTORY OF OUR DESIRES
WOLFGANG SACHS, 1992, 227 PAGES, HARD COVER

Far more than a means of transport, the automobile has become a cultural icon for our times. Examining the history of the automobile from the late 1880s to the present, Sachs shows how the car gave form to the dreams and desires embedded in modern society—for speed, independence, comfort, status, glamour and power—and in so doing reshaped our very notions of time and space, our individual and societal values, and our outlook on progress and the future. In sum: an excellent and detailed cultural history of the car.

THE GEOGRAPHY OF NOWHERE
THE RISE AND DECLINE OF
AMERICA'S MAN-MADE LANDSCAPE
JAMES HOWARD KUNSTLER, 1994, 304 PP.

Explores and deplores the privatized suburban wasteland that makes up so much of North America today. Not the most technical book on the subject of sprawl, but certainly one of the most entertaining, passionate, readable and accessible. One of the most popular books on the subject. The predecessor to Home from Nowhere.

HOME FROM NOWHERE
REMAKING OUR EVERYDAY WORLD FOR THE 21ST CENTURY
JAMES HOWARD KUNSTLER, 1998, 320 PAGES

Kunstler offers a way back from the "tragic sprawlscape of cartoon architecture, junked cities, and ravaged countryside" that he described in The Geography of Nowhere. He calls for the restoration of traditional architecture, sensible urban design principles, and the development of public spaces that meet people's need to interact with one another.

LIFE BETWEEN BUILDINGS
JAN GEHL, 2001, 202 PAGES, FOURTH ENGLISH EDITION

A classic is republished and revised. First published in 1971, this book is still the best source for understanding how people use public spaces. Published in many languages, it is a standard textbook in architecture and planning schools around the world, and continues to be the undisputed introduction to the interplay between public space design and social life. It will forever change the way you look at the urban environment.

THE LITTLE DRIVER
MARTIN WAGNER, 2003, 56 PAGES

Joe always dreamt of driving his own car. When his wish comes true and he takes his brand-new sports car for a spin, his adventures soon take a turn for the unexpected. A children's book for young and old, The Little Driver takes a fresh look at our obsession with cars through the eyes of a boy still young enough to take nothing for granted.

NEW CITY SPACES
JAN GEHL AND LARS GEMZOE, 2001, 263 PAGES

Through color photos, descriptive text and diagrams, this informative book highlights 39 public spaces around the world that have been won back from traffic.

STREET RECLAIMING
CREATING LIVABLE STREETS AND VIBRANT COMMUNITIES
DAVID ENGWICHT, 1999, 207 PAGES

Street Reclaiming not only celebrates the potential of our streets to become vibrant centres of culture and community once again—but also shows you how you can make it happen. A leap beyond traffic calming, the book contains a host of practical ideas and tools for reclaiming your streets.

SUSTAINABILITY & CITIES
OVERCOMING AUTOMOBILE DEPENDENCE
PETER NEWMAN AND JEFF KENWORTHY, 1999, 350 PP.

This book makes the case that the essential character of a city's land use results from how it manages transport, and that only by reducing our automobile dependence will we be able to successfully accommodate the full sustainability agenda. The authors provide a survey of global cities using a range of sustainability factors and indicators, and demonstrate how cities around the world are overcoming automobile dependence.

ALSO FROM CAR BUSTERS PRESS

ROADKILL BILL　　　　　　**by KEN AVIDOR**

WORLD CARFREE NETWORK WORKS TO **BUILD** AND MAINTAIN THE GLOBAL CARFREE MOVEMENT. ITS PROJECTS AND PUBLICATIONS **ASSIST** PEOPLE AROUND THE WORLD **TAKING ON** CAR CULTURE AND PROMOTING ALTERNATIVE WAYS OF LIFE. WE AIM TO **FACILITATE EXCHANGE** AND **COOPERATION** AMONG ACTIVISTS AND CAMPAIGNERS, REACH OUT TO THE PUBLIC, **INSPIRE** NEW ACTIVISTS AND **CHANGE THE WORLD**.

ANDY'S THANK YOU'S:

I wish to give thanks and love to my father, who loved trains and mass transit and who was always supportive of my cartoon and artistic endeavors. Thank you to my mom, my spouse Cara, Jane Holtz Kay, Katie Alvord and Mark O'Lalor for helping me proofread and edit the text. Many thanks to Randy Ghent—activist, super desktop publisher, co-editor of Car Busters and former editor of Auto-Free Times. Without him, this book and many of its cartoons would never have been made.

Thank you to Oregon Cycling, Transportation Alternatives, Car Busters, and Jan Lundberg (former publisher of Auto-Free Times) for using my CARtoons and inspiring me to draw more of them. Thanks to Mo and Dan for their love and invaluable computer assistance.

And thanks to all the amazing activists I've met or talked to who have inspired me to try and do the right thing: David Nadel, David Brower and Jonathan Montague (may they rest in peace), Kathy Simmonds, the Planck family, Jennifer Margulis di Properzio, David Cohen, Stephen Dunnifer, Autumn Buss, Matt Wuerker and many others.